The
HOVENSA
Chronicles
By
Valerie
Knowles
Combie

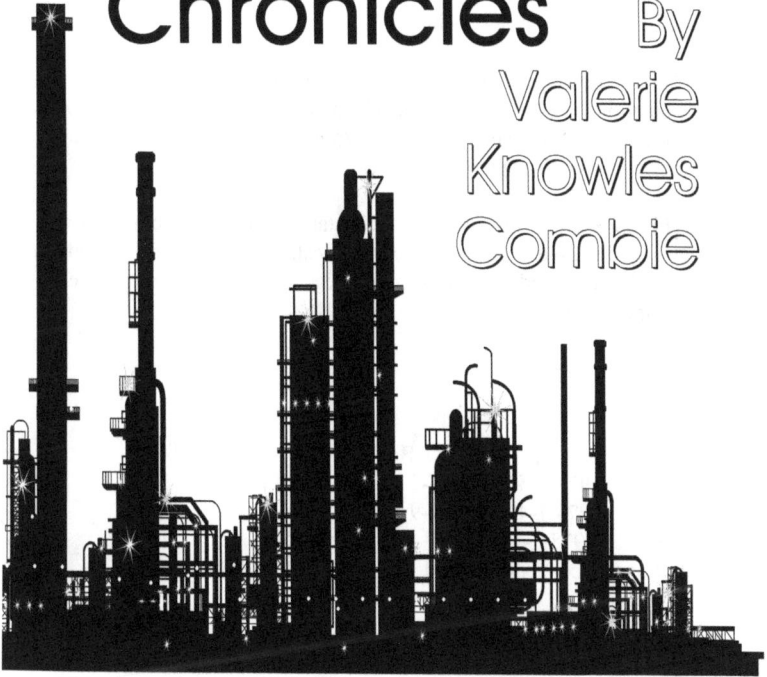

AB **ASPECT Books**
www.ASPECTBooks.com

Copyright © 2013 ASPECT Books
ISBN-13: 978-1-4796-0245-2 (Paperback)
ISBN-13: 978-1-4796-0246-9 (ePub)
ISBN-13: 978-1-4796-0247-6 (Kindle/Mobi)
Library of Congress Control Number: 2013913354

Published by

AB ASPECT Books
www.ASPECTBooks.com

Table of Contents

Introduction

HOVENSA, formerly known also the Hess Oil Refinery, the Hess Oil Virgin Islands Corporation (HOVIC), or the St. Croix Refinery is a petroleum refinery located on the island of St. Croix in the United States Virgin Islands. After the owner, Leon Hess died, the refinery became a joint venture between Hess Corporation and Petroleos de Venezuela, hence the name HOVENSA. For most of its operating life as HOVENSA it supplied heating oil and gasoline to the U.S. Gulf Coast and the eastern seaboard with the crude mainly sourced from Venezuela. Previously it had sourced its crude feedstock from a number of other countries including Libya. At a capacity of about 500,000 barrels per day as of 2010 it was in the top 10 largest refineries in the world.

Hess Oil Virgin Islands Corporation started refinery construction in January

1966 having purchased the property from Annie de Chabert, and in October of the same year, the refinery started operating. In 1974, the capacity of refinery was expanded up to its peak at 650,000 barrels per day. HOVENSA LLC, which took over the refinery operatorship, was established in 1998. In January 2011, HOVENSA paid a $5.3 million penalty for Clean Air Act violations.

On January 18, 2012 the company announced that it would close the refinery by mid-February 2012. The refinery will then serve as a storage terminal.

"The HOVENSA Chronicles" attempts to document the impact of the closing of the oil refinery on the United States Virgin Islands, primarily St. Croix.

Part I: Breaking News

Breaking news rocks the airways
But no one believes
It's just another bit of shocking news
That shatters the peace
The metaphoric straw
But this camel's back is not broken
It may be shaken,
But not broken.
This community has been overcharged
Overtaxed
Overwhelmed
With too many demands
And too little resources.

But then reality strikes.
HOVENSA WILL CLOSE! $1.3 billion lost
Oil refining a thing of the past
HOVENSA WILL CLOSE
Resulting in "wide-spread anxiety
And speculations across the Territory,"

Reports *The Daily News.*
In retrospect, there were the clues
But we were lulled into complacency
Doubting the mega plant's insolvency
Not in our lifetimes, we said
Failing to adhere to the trend.

Two thousand people will lose their jobs
Families will lose incomes
Schools will lose students
Businesses will lose patrons
Organizations will lose support
The government will lose millions
Which will be our loss as well
How will we survive?
How can such a small island
Absorb such great losses?
Resulting in the winter
Spring
Summer
And fall of our discontent
As the refinery
Octopus-like
Spreads its tentacles
Touching each life
Invading each family

Spewing its venom and misery
While union leaders stand helpless
With no official word
For their flocks.

In its glory days
Hess
HOVIC – Hess Oil Virgin Islands
    Corporation
HOVENSA, one of the world's largest
    oil refineries
Enriched thousands
Supported the Virgin Islands
Kept St. Croix running
Like a greased engine
Keeping the machine producing
Greasing the palms
Of millions.

HOVENSA refined 500,000 barrels of
    oil per day
That brought wealth
To thousands along the way
But after exploring "all available options"
To keep the refinery open
The losses forced the decisions

Low price of natural gas
Severe financial losses
EPA and the Department of Justice's
    charges
Decreasing demands for refined
    petroleum products
Increasing new refining capacity
It was not feasible
To continue the hemorrhaging.
To recoup its losses
Was impossible.
HOVENSA is closing in phases
To end the forty-six year relationship.

The question remains
How will we survive?
Is there life after HOVENSA?

Part II:
And the Lights
Went Out

From a distance
The stream of lights creates
A panoramic display
Transforming St. Croix's southeastern
    horizon
All-seeing eyes
Dominate the landscape
Monarchs of all they survey
Red lights
Amber lights
And sometimes green
Beckoning to the fulfillment
Of the American dream
Here in the Virgin Islands
Lights reflecting the opulence
Concealing the impermanence
Of life's abundance
Tonight their presence
Mocks the reality

Of the losses sustained
Through a global recession
That drains our economy.

Beaming lights a symbol
Of the Hess Oil Virgin Islands
    Corporation
Touching lives
Creating jobs
Providing for families
Supporting local organizations
Extending scholarships and other
    educational opportunities
Assisting with programs
Donating money
Expertise
Time
Labor
Buildings
Furniture
Supplies
A philanthropic corporate citizen
Creating opportunities for thousands
Enhancing lives
Resulting in improved standard of living
Expanded worldviews.

The lights have been glowing
A symbolic image of permanence
With the volcanic flue
From the smoke stacks
Now only a memory.

How much longer must we wait
Before those lights will be gone?
What will be the result
Of a transfomed landscape?
Will the absent lights
Reflect our interrupted dreams?
Will the promise of enhanced lives
Be a "dream deferred"?
Will the south shore become a specter
Of the glory days of HOVENSA?
The former bustling housing complexes
Constant traffic at the Rec Hall
People eating
Children milling around
Over-flowing on to the grounds
Playing tennis
Basketball
Walking
Running
Screaming

Enjoying a healthy atmosphere
Where parents
Employers
Guests
And children gathered
To socialize
To relax
To unwind
To affirm life.

Those days are gone
Only a lingering memory
Of what used to be
A life style taken for granted
By a populace
Believing that HOVENSA was Gibraltar
An unassailable rock
Impregnable
And constant as the North Star
Glowing its permanence
Lighting the way
Exuding warm complacency
Engendering abandon and profligacy
Now resulting in wasted time
Wasted effort
Wasted resources

Decadence.
Will the diminishing lights
Beckon us forward
To a great reality
And renewed exploration
Of possibilities
That could have been
But are now too late?

Will the lights still be there
Tomorrow
Next week
Next year
Another decade?

How will the Territory survive
The absence of the lights?

The south-eastern sky is still lit
Though sparsely
Areas once aflame
Are now dark
Gone is the smoke of the flue
Now cold and bare
Each night more lights disappear.

Will they ever be rekindled?
Will they resurrect
Heralding the birth of a new era?
Or have they sung their swan song
The dirge of a period long gone?

Will the memories of the lights
Rekindle the dreams
Now vanished from our sight?
Will those diminishing lights
Dampen our spirits
Destroy our hope
In the future?

The remaining lights flicker
Not unlike a candle
Whose flame flickers in the wind
Twisting this way and that
Bending
Bowing
Dancing
Gyrating
But not being extinguished
Until the final piece
Having given its last glow
Is burnt down

Burnt out
Engulfed by melted wax
It struggles
Flickers
Dies
Do the absent lights
Herald its death?

Alas! Other lights burning brightly
Once overshadowed by the greater lights
Now assert themselves
Shining brighter
Warmer
Beckoning to a future
Restoring the promise
Of permanence
In a quasi-permanent world
Rekindling the hope
Of our deferred dreams
Reminding us that
"Hope springs eternal"
To those who trust
In the greater message
The permanent promise
Of fulfilled dreams.

Does each light symbolize
A life
An employee
Whose years of service
Will end abruptly?

Many business ventures have preceded
    HOVENSA:
Barker's
Franklin's
Carib Air
Prinair
Eastern Airline
PANAM Airline
Harvey
Martin Marietta
Woolworth
Cavanaughs
Continental
CIGNA Insurance
Little Switzerland
They came
They thrived
They left
But we remained
Picking up the pieces

Carrying on
Like the Phoenix
We rise from the ashes
Of our burnt desires
Scorched dreams
Torched hopes
We experience the pain
The fear of losses
Desperation.

The remaining lights flicker
Exposing the dark spots
Created by the absent lights
Resurrecting the dreams
Restoring hope
For the future
A future of uncertainties
Denied possibilities
And more uncertainties.

From a distance
The landscape looks different
Those once beaming lights
Are now at rest
Snuffed out
Their mandated tasks

Have been completed.
Extinguished
Interrupted
No longer do they transform
The south-eastern landscape
No longer do they command
The horizon
Guarding the skies
Alerting planes
Guiding tankers into its port
Providing a livelihood for workers.

Will they all be snuffed out?
Or will some remain
As a reminder
A bearer
Of hope
For our long-lost dreams
Rekindled in the gleams
Of the lights?

They may decrease in number
But they will remain
Transferring HOVENSA
Into its next phase
Reduced lights

Reduced demands
Reduced manpower
Reduced income
Reduced involvement
Reduced output
Reduced losses
To whom?
For whom?
Don't we all lose?

Part III: Reflections

Those were the days!
Construction of houses
Offices
Facilities
To accommodate workers
Who arrived in droves
By air
By land
By sea
Hess is hiring
Skilled workers required
Bringing an influx of immigrants
From other Caribbean islands
English
French
Dutch
Creole
Papiamento
Spanish
Regional dialects
Single men
Men with their families

Contractors
Operators
Janitors
Caterers
Secretaries
Service providers
Of all nations
Classes
Creeds
Ethnicities
Converged on St. Croix
Building a new plant
Major undertaking
But not impossible
Employing the skilled and unskilled
Creating a boom
Which must result in a bust
But who thinks of the future
At the inception
Of a transformation
Of an island
A Territory
A life?
The future is now
Seize the jobs
Capture compensation

Surpassing expectation
In the exploitation
Of an industry
That will transform people
Influencing thousands
Who have risked much
But what's to lose?
"Walk about fool is better than sit
    down fool"
Say the elders
Whose lives have been built on risks
People leaving children
Wives
Husbands
Parents
Friends
Seeking a new life
A new beginning
Sacrificing much
Experiencing privation
Exploitation
Separation
Isolation
Alienation
Working for the Yankee dollar
To build houses

Repay debts
Sponsorships
Loyalties
Securing the coveted green card
Another step toward naturalization
And United States citizenship.

Another wave of immigrants
Children
Parents
Yet more workers
Entombed in the bowels
Of the fast-growing plant
Suffocating
Chewing up
Grinding down
Swallowing
Ultimately spitting out
Broken men and women
Now prosperous
Surrounded by material wealth
But broken in spirit and health
Unfair labor practices
Injustices
Of a system
An institution

That determines one's worth
By his color, his birth
Not by his production
Assembly line fashion
Demanding more
More
More
And yet more
Inhumane taskmasters
Applying the metaphoric whip
Making the token promotion
Engendering contention
Segregation
In a naïve community
With the chosen secured behind
    barbed wire fences
Shutting our those
Keeping in these
The privileged
Creating rancor
Among those who compete to enter
To be classified
With the favored.

It was hard work
Back-breaking work

Unrelenting hours
Demanding supers
Testing the powers
Mind racking
But pay day was coming
A bitter sweet day of reckoning
Nor knowing a coworker's pay
Forbidden to say
But therein the ambiguity lay
The pay was greater
In the Territory no better
Spelling untold wealth
Translated into a secure future
With money well spent.

Alas! "All that glitters is not gold"
We have been told
"The fool and his money are soon parted"
We did behold
As wine, women, and song
Robbed many of their goals
Of improved family condition
Breaking up homes
Creating unforeseen situations
On a little island
Surfeiting on overabundance

And uncontrolled spending.

Shopping mass resulted
From the newly found wealth
And quickly grown population
Accommodating a new lifestyle
New stores followed
Private schools proliferated
To ease the burden of public schools
And accommodate paying parents
Investing in their children's education
Simultaneously showing their new status
Securing new alliances
New commitments
For a new breed of people
 With a new focus
New future
Unlimited possibilities.

New businesses
Banks
Stores
Groceries
Gas stations
Proliferate
Followed by

Bars
Restaurants
Service industries
Transforming a quiet place
Into a booming
Thriving metropolis
Centerline tree lined
Boasting its stores
Shopping malls
Businesses.

Part IV:
The Exodus

The lights on the southeastern horizon
    are diminishing.
Many yellow orbs have disappeared
Leaving the dark spots
Interspersed with red blinking lights
Precursors of the future
Uncertain
Incomprehensible
Unknown.

But all is not dark
There glimmers a light
 The light of hope
Springing eternal each day each night
Evoking memories of times past
Entertaining reflection

The legal requirement
Of ninety days
Seemed such a long time

But, indeed, it was too short
Time to dismantle the plant
Store sensitive parts in cotton balls
Dispose of others
Selling
Trading
Discarding
Donating
Auctioning
How do you undo forty-six years' labor
In ninety days?

How do you dismantle a plant
In ninety days?
Can forty-six years be auctioned
In ninety days?
The varying areas
East Refinery
West Refinery
Coker Plant
How do they downsize?
Will the selected hundred
Get lost in the plant
Or will the storage be restricted?
How does a mind
Understand a plan

From two thousand to a hundred
In just ninety days?
What time do you allow
For reminiscences
Reflections
Holding on to treasured moments
And those trophies
That rekindle memories
Of success
Victory
Great insight?
How do you hold back the floodgates
Washing over the senses
Overwhelming the emotions
Resulting in tears
Tears of regret
Longing
Lost plans
Dashed hopes
Of seeing children's future betrayed
By forces over which they have no
    control
Do you ever see men bawl?
Not a pretty sight.

Men weep internally

For the interruptions of their lives
The test of their manhood
The ability to provide
They are the breadwinners
We've been told
They bring home the gold
Creating images of wealth
That are only an illusion.

Men bawl for the jobs they've lost
Jobs with compensation
That had spoiled them
Where can they earn such mega
      salaries?
How will they maintain their families
Who will tell the children
That the money is restricted
And the style of living limited?

Will they understand
Or will their pampered lives
Prevent the penetration of reality?
Will they vent their
Resentment
Disappointment
Disillusionment

Betrayal?
Or will they grow up
Accept
And apply themselves?

April 20 was the last day for many
It's been done
The masses are gone
The HOVENSA Oil Refinery
Is history.

And the lights reflect
That history
The southeastern horizon is dark
With large dark spots
Emptiness
A precursor of the state of our Territory
And the void created
By a confluence of factors
Leaving only a memory
Of what used to be.

The yellow lights have diminished
Leaving no traces
Of a once vibrant place
Illuminating the landscape

Creating energy and warmth
With promises of future dreams
And plans unfulfilled.

The remaining red lights
Blink on and off
On and off
On and off
Will they continue to blink?
Can they discern what we think?
Will they continue
On and off
On and off
Or will they soon be permanently off?
Feelings of fear
Insecurity
Linger near
Uncertainties replace our dreams
No longer are we sure, it seems
When once the bottom falls out
It creates much doubt
And we border on paranoia
Leading to hysteria
Who will occupy vacated houses
Apartments
Villas

Hotel rooms
And condominiums?
Who will patronize restaurants
Health clubs
Casinos
And races?
And the schools—
How will they survive?
How will we thrive
In a depleted economy?

Part V:
The Aftermath

Has it been only forty-six years
When such plans created fears
Challenged the status quo
And introduced
The legislative bill
That would transform St. Croix's south
    shore
Aye, the whole Territory?

Did we ignore the writing on the wall
Failed to study
The history of oil refineries
Whose life expectancy was determined
Not by longevity
But by economy
And demands for the product?

Were we cloaked in denial
Afraid to observe the trends
Of the global recession

Wreaking havoc
Or were we blinded by our complacency
Unable or unwilling to agree
With Goldman Sachs' intimation
Of the termination?

Has reality struck
Or are we coaxing Lady Luck
Hoping that we'll awake
From our dream
And the nightmare that makes
Us scream?
Awake!
It is true!
Hess Oil Refinery
Our HOVENSA
No longer exists
The transition team
Has begun its work
Working diligently
No time to shirk
Its responsibility
And present a reduced facility
To compete in a market
Where only the strongest survive.
Will the reduced labor force

Adequately meet the demands
Of the new designation
Of a storage facility?
Will the plant expand
Or will it fail to thrive
In a new economy?
Who will silence the voices
Of the ghosts of HOVENSA past?
Who will apply the tourniquet
To staunch the bleeding
Of a people
An island
A Territory
That is ricocheting into bankruptcy
Not only economically
Educationally
Psychologically
Socially
Spiritually.

Can we arise
Dust ourselves off
Pick up the pieces
And move on?
How resilient are we?
Or are we too battered

To get up and do battle
Not for ourselves
But for posterity
Can we bear the privation
The diminished expectations
And sacrifice
So that our children
Can be guaranteed
A secure future?

Part VI:
Lessons Learned

The diminished lights
Have transformed the southeastern
    landscape
No longer do they portray
That reassuring feeling
Of permanence
Security
And prosperity.
In their absence
The void creates darkness
Interspersed with the red lights
That symbolize
A cessation
Of motion
A brief pause
A halt
An interrupted dream
That has changed plans
Lives
Lifestyles

The future.

The lights have presaged
Diminished traffic
Locked, empty parking lots
Absent people
Former employees
Whose tenure with HOVENSA
Has ended
Some of whom have been forced into
    retirement
Unemployed
But not useless
Others have moved on to other jobs
Relocated
Fractured families
Uncertain futures
Indecisions
But the will remains
To surmount the odds.

What will the future present?
How will we meet obligations?
How will we establish foundations
For our youth, our future?

Will the red lights
Pause us permanently?
Will the young understand sacrifice?
Children whose every wish
Has been met
Spoiled with life's toys
Gimmicks
Fashions
That produce temporary joys
Until a greater
Better
Costlier
Toy emerges
Creating greater demands
Intense urges
That must be satisfied?

Will they rise to the challenge
Embrace the changes
And demonstrate the resilience
Of our ancestors
That enabled them to overcome
All odds
Survive the brutality
Ultimately triumphed over inhumanity
And forged a life

That defied history
Creating a destiny
And a path
Where we can follow
Stepping in the footsteps
Imprinted with pain
Sweat
And tears
Stained with the blood
That flowed profusely
As their lives ebbed away
Only to be continued by others
Who understood the true meaning of
    sacrifice?
They sacrificed their lives
So that we can bask
In life's pursuits
They were denied
The pursuit of happiness
Family life
Education
Choice.
Those who were robbed of their choices
Chose to sacrifice their lives
So that we could pursue happiness
Those who were denied an education

Knew its benefits
Understood its road to upward mobility
Success
And progress
Sacrificed their future
So that we could enjoy the rights of an
    education.

Those who were denied the institution
    of the family
One of society's primary institutions
The cradle of socialization
Emotional stability
Spiritual and physical maturity
Longed through their brokenness
To establish homes
Where love
Unity
And respect
Would nurture and mold children
Into contributing members of society
But those thoughts were thwarted
By an oppressive system
That catered to domination
And greed
Feeding on a people's subjugation

Suppression
Oppression
Molestation
Isolation
Proposed extermination

But our ancestors stood resolute
Backs bent under the load
Of brutal beatings
Forced abductions
And concubinage
But hearts firm and stalwart
Determined and unbent
Pressing on
Faces scarred but focused
Eyes on the future
Unobstructed by the oppressive system
Devoid of restrictions
Enforced by pigmentation
Sacrificed their lives
So that we could create families
Who would build our societies.

Those who were robbed of their
    "inalienable rights
To life

Liberty
And the pursuit of happiness"
Had no rights
Did not own their lives
And were enslaved
In an oppressive system
That eliminated any pursuit of
    happiness.
They sacrificed all
To ensure the continuation of the race
A noble people created in God's image
Endowed with intellect
Sensitivity to others
And the ability to enact changes
Scientists of the highest caliber
Physicians
Architects
Engineers
Artistes and artisans
Scholars
Diplomats
A people of highest aspirations
Demonstrated through their
    accomplishments.

The sacrifice was not in vain.

Only temporarily interrupted
 By hundreds of years of exploitation
But their race
Not unlike the children of Israel
Who suffered through Egyptian bondage
Were liberated through divine
     intervention
Were emancipated
Their rights reinstated
But they ignored the sacrifice.

They will learn sacrifice
If only through the scientific principles
That "force makes water go up hill"
And life continues still
But only the strong survive.
They will apply those principles
Of sacrifice
That through the lives
Of our ancestors
Basic principles of living within our
     means
Foregoing wants and desires
And attempts to compete
In a race that is replete
With overtones of insecurity

Jealousy
Greed and
Denial
They will sacrifice pleasures
For the more lasting benefits
Of education
And building on the foundation
Laid in anticipation
Of the continuity of the race.

HOVENSA's transformation
Is only a hiatus
A hiccup in the systemic plan
Of a people whose resilience
Will propel them on to succeed
Where others would have failed
They will suck the salt of
    disappointment
Eat the widi widi bush for sustenance
With their eyes focused on the goal
And their backs slightly bent
But their hearts resolute and intent
Forging on to embrace this opportunity
Presented by HOVENSA
To assert themselves
Accept responsibility for their lives

And carve that new society
Predicted by our ancestors
Whose sacrifices have not been in vain.

We will survive
St. Croix will arise and thrive
The Territory will rebound
From the temporary loss
Because we are the children of survivors
We are the products of phenomenal
        sacrifices
We are an invincible race
Of salt suckers
Widi widi bush eaters
Water drinkers.
We need only the basics
And though spoiled by the taste of honey
And overabundance of money
We will resort to our inherited tendencies
We will relearn the lessons of our
        ancestors
And we will sacrifice
So that our children will inherit a future
Unspoilt by restrictions
Limitations
Or self-imposed boundaries

We may retreat temporarily
But advance we must
With hearts resolute
Eyes focused on the goal
And the purpose unimpeded by change.

Part VII:
Moving Forward

The HOVENSA Refinery is closed
Employees have been paid
Some have relocated to new jobs
Others have returned to school
And still others have retired.
The plant continues its new phase
Of a greatly reduced crew
Preparing for the transition
By mothballing the plant
Only to be reduced to a few
By the end of July.

Interviewers have arrived on island
Luring our men and women
To other plants in other places
Alabama
Alaska
Florida
Texas
Yet others are tempted by the lures of

Saudi Arabia
Abu Dhabi
Will they succumb to the temptation?
Will pride of manhood
Force them to sell their souls
For highly tempting salaries
Under oppressive administrations
Where their democratic wills
Struggle with fundamentalist fervor
That restricts their inhibitions
Challenges their constitutions
Confuses their minds
And breaks their spirits?

The road through the plant is deserted
Practically abandoned
With the greatly reduced traffic
Gone is the impatient blowing of horns
Flashing of lights
Long lines of vehicles
Anxiously exiting the parking lots
Escaping from the refinery
Whose stench clings to the coveralls
Invading the vehicle's interior
Contaminating the homes
As one shift departs and another enters

The silence of absent vehicles
Reverberates through the air
With its impatient revving of engines
Loud outbursts from high-powered
     motorcycles
Bobbing and weaving through traffic
Performing dare-devil stunts
Defying the laws of gravity
Exposing the timid of heart.

The parking lots are padlocked
Closed
Empty
Ghost lots
With grass growing in spots
Moving on to abandonment
And disuse
While the potholes on the road grow
     bigger.
A smaller crew continued
Until December
Cleaning tanks
Pipelines
Preparing the plant for the next phase.
The new venture
Of an oil storage facility

Run by the transition team
Of 100.
How did they arrive at that number?
How were the chosen selected?
Was there a lottery
Or were they hand picked?

What will be the fate of the camps
The housing units?
Estate Hope
Estate Fig Tree
Estate Blessing
Estate Cottage?

Will mobile units be destroyed
By demolition crews
Annihilating homes
Erasing lives and memories?
Who will inhabit the houses
Or walk on streets lined with trees
Surrounded by manicured lawns
And well landscaped terraces?

There are so many unanswered
    questions
But time moves on

And the future is now
Portraying the loss
In closed businesses
Escalating gas prices
Reduced services
Layoffs
More reductions
Anything to staunch the bleeding
Of a negative cashflow.

Yet, the commitments remain:
Property taxes
WAPA bills
Other utility bills
Mortgages
Car payments
Credit card bills
Other debts
More demands on limited funds
How do we decide
Whom to pay?
What priority measure
Comes into play
When we must decide between debts
      or food
WAPA or medication?

What a quandary!

As we decide
The crime rate increases
Robbers wax bolder
The weapons grow deadlier
Penetrating the bullet-proof vests
Of peace officers
As more bodies are left to die
Strewn on streets
Worse than dogs
Or common vermin.

Life is no longer valued
Its sanctity dismissed
And daily the funeral train

Moves along
Reminding us of another senseless death
A mother's heart broken
And children cringe
In the face of a terror
Without a face
But with a name.

How will the changes

Affect our lives?
Will we assert ourselves
And determine our fate
Or will we lie down and play dead
And realize too late
That we determine our destiny
We are the captains of our fate?

And so we move on
Resolute in our decisions
Determined to bravely face the torrents
Swimming valiantly against the tide
Of economic and social upheavals.

We invite you to view the complete
selection of titles we publish at:

www.AspectBooks.com

Scan with your mobile
device to go directly
to our website.

Please write or email us your praises, reactions, or
thoughts about this or any other book we publish at:

AB **ASPECT Books**
www.ASPECTBooks.com

P.O. Box 954
Ringgold, GA 30736

info@AspectBooks.com

Aspect Books titles may be purchased in bulk for
educational, business, fund-raising,
or sales promotional use.
For information, please e-mail

BulkSales@AspectBooks.com

Finally, if you are interested in seeing
your own book in print, please contact us at

publishing@AspectBooks.com

We would be happy to review your manuscript for free.

www.ingramcontent.com/pod-product-compliance
Lightning Source LLC
Chambersburg PA
CBHW060809110426
42739CB00032BA/3157